1st GRADE
READING COMPREHENSION

📖 Read the story.　　❓ Read each question.
🔍 Find answers in the story.　　✏️ Write your answers.

Rex's New Dog

Rex got a new dog. He loves to play
dog. Sometimes Rex takes his dog to
park. They run and jump and chase
other. Rex throws a ball for his dog.
Rex has fun with his new dog!

1. What did Rex get?
_____

2. What does Rex love to do?
_____

3. Where does Rex take his dog?
_____

📖 Read the story.　　❓ Read each question.
🔍 Find answers in the story.　　✏️ Write your answers.

A Snowy Day

It is snowy and cold. Jen wants to go outside
and play. She has to get ready first. Jen goes
to her room to get her boots. Next, Jen puts
on a hat and her coat. Now Jen is ready to
go out and play in the snow.

1. Where does Jen want to go?
_____

2. What is the weather?
_____

3. Where are Jen's boots?
_____

📖 Read the story.　　❓ Read each question.
d answers in the story.　　✏️ Write your answers.

Party at the Park

y is my birthday. I will have a party at
ark. The park is a good place for a party.
riends can run and play. We can have
on the picnic bench. All the moms and
can sit and talk. A park is the best
for a party.

ere can we have cake?
_____

o can run and play?
_____

y am I having a party at the park?
_____

A WORKBOOK TO BUILD
BEGINNING READ SKILLS

ISBN: 979-8-86960771-3

First printing edition 2023.

10 9 8 7 6 5 4 3 2 1

Published in Ormond Beach, Florida.

Contact the author :
fishyrobb.com

TABLE OF CONTENTS

www.fishyrobb.com

How to Use This Book

Reading is more than just sounding out the words on a page. Children must also understand what the words mean. This workbook is designed to give first graders many opportunities to build that understanding and develop important comprehension skills as they read stories on their level.

There are eight different short stories in this workbook. Before each, you will see a list of "Words to Practice" that you should review with your child. These are sight words that cannot be easily sounded out. If your child knows and can read these words, they are ready for the whole story.

After the story, there are three comprehension questions. Your child may be able to answer them by recalling what they just read, or by going back to find the answers in the text. I suggest having students underline where they found the answer in the story.

Finally, there is a Main Idea and Details cut-and-paste chart for each story. Identifying the main idea is an important skill that is taught in all elementary grades and requires a lot of practice. After reading the story, have your child cut out the three statements and glue them onto the chart to show which is the main idea and which two are the supporting details. If your child struggles with this concept, help by rereading the story together and talking about the "Big Idea" versus all the tiny extra bits that help us understand it. Remember, the supporting details give us more specific information about the main idea.

STORY 1
Rex's New Dog

Words to Practice

new

loves

play

they

other

Read the story. Read each question.

Find answers in the story. Write your answers.

Rex's New Dog

Rex got a new dog. He loves to play with his dog. Sometimes Rex takes his dog to the park. They run and jump and chase each other. Rex throws a ball for his dog. Rex has fun with his new dog!

1. What did Rex get?

_____

2. What does Rex love to do?

_____

3. Where does Rex take his dog?

_____

Think about the story. What was the most important idea?

Main Idea

(the most important thing the author wants you to know)

Details

(tells more about the main idea)

(tells more about the main idea)

Directions:

 Cut out the statements.

 Glue them on the chart above to show which is the main idea and which are details..

Rex loves to play with his dog.

They run and jump and chase each other.

Rex throws a ball for his dog.

STORY 2
A Snowy Day

Words to Practice

cold

wants

ready

goes

puts

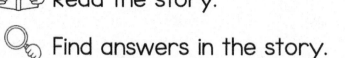 Read the story.

 Read each question.

Find answers in the story.

Write your answers.

A Snowy Day

It is snowy and cold. Jen wants to go outside and play. She has to get ready first. Jen goes to her room to get her boots. Next, Jen puts on a hat and her coat. Now Jen is ready to go out and play in the snow.

---

1. Where does Jen want to go?

_____

- -

_____

2. What is the weather?

_____

- -

_____

3. Where are Jen's boots?

_____

- -

_____

A Snowy Day

It is snowy and cold. Jen wants to go outside and play. She has to get ready first. Jen goes to her room to get her boots. Next, her puts on her hat and her coat. Now Jen is ready to go out and play in the snow.

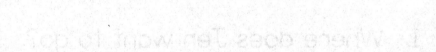

1. Where does Jen want to go?

_____

_____

2. What is the weather?

_____

_____

3. Where are Jen's boots?

_____

_____

Think about the story. What was the most important idea?

Main Idea

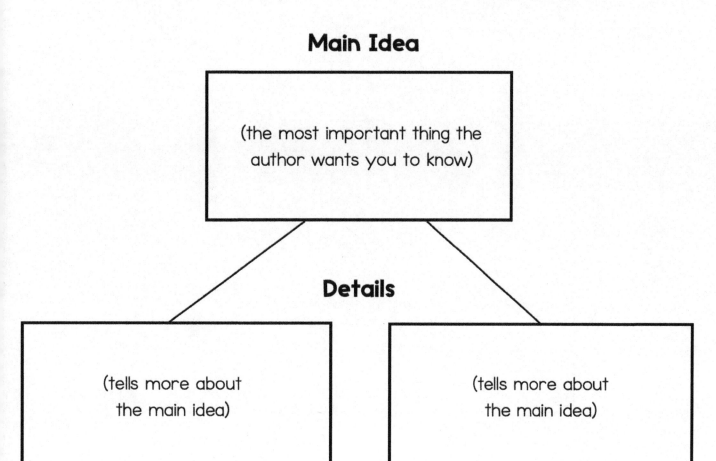

(the most important thing the author wants you to know)

Details

(tells more about the main idea)

(tells more about the main idea)

Directions:

 Cut out the statements.

 Glue them on the chart above to show which is the main idea and which are details..

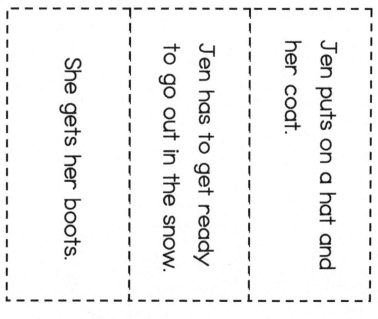

She gets her boots.

Jen has to get ready to go out in the snow.

Jen puts on a hat and her coat.

STORY 3
Party At the Park

Words to Practice

today

have

place

friends

talk

📖 Read the story.　　❓ Read each question.

🔍 Find answers in the story.　　✎ Write your answers.

Party at the Park

Today is my birthday. I will have a party at the park. The park is a good place for a party. My friends can run and play. We can have cake on the picnic bench. All the moms and dads can sit and talk. A park is the best place for a party.

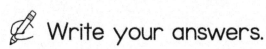

1.　Where can we have cake?

　　_____

　　- -

　　_____

2.　Who can run and play?

　　_____

　　- -

　　_____

3.　Why am I having a party at the park?

　　_____

　　- -

　　_____

Think about the story. What was the most important idea?

Main Idea

(the most important thing the author wants you to know)

Details

(tells more about the main idea)

(tells more about the main idea)

- -

Directions:

 Cut out the statements.

 Glue them on the chart above to show which is the main idea and which are details..

The park is a good place for a party.

My friends can run and play.

We can have cake on the picnic bench.

STORY 4
The Blue House

Words to Practice

Mr.

Mrs.

they

some

blue

The Blue House

Mr. and Mrs. Tam had a green house. They do not like green. They wanted to paint the house. Mr. Tam went and got some paint. Mrs. Tam went and got some brushes. They painted all day. Now the house is blue!

1. What did Mr. and Mrs. Tam want to do?

   _____

   _

   _____

2. What did Mr. Tam get?

   _____

   _

   _____

3. What color is the house now?

   _____

   _

   _____

Think about the story. What was the most important idea?

Main Idea

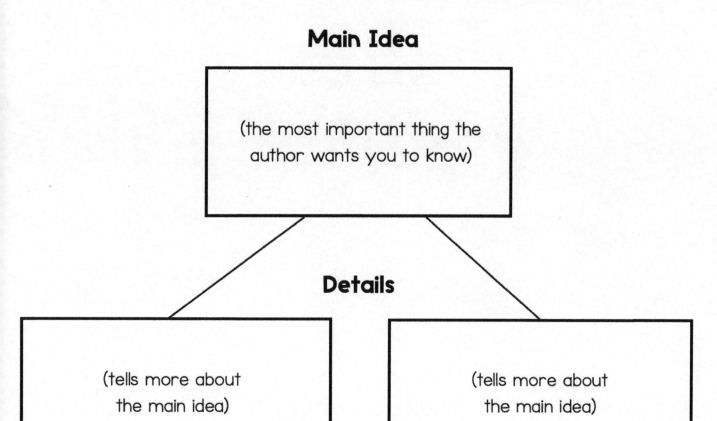

(the most important thing the author wants you to know)

Details

(tells more about the main idea)

(tells more about the main idea)

Directions:

 Cut out the statements.

 Glue them on the chart above to show which is the main idea and which are details..

Mrs. Tam went and got some brushes.

Mr. Tam went and got some paint.

Mr. and Mrs. Tam wanted to paint the house.

STORY 5
Lost Cat

Words to Practice

was

animal

give

some

ready

find

Lost Cat

Jax is a little, black cat. He was lost. The animal shelter is taking care of him. The workers give Jax a bath and some food. The vet looks at him to see if he is sick. Jax gets a shot. Now Jax is clean and well. He is ready to find a new home.

1. Who is taking care of Jax?

_____

2. Why does the vet look at Jax?

_____

3. What color is Jax?

_____

Think about the story. What was the most important idea?

Main Idea

(the most important thing the author wants you to know)

Details

(tells more about the main idea)

(tells more about the main idea)

Directions:

 Cut out the statements.

 Glue them on the chart above to show which is the main idea and which are details..

The workers give Jax a bath and some food.

The animal shelter is taking care of Jax.

The vet looks at him to see if he is sick.

STORY 6
A Day At the Farm

<u>Words to Practice</u>

lives

are

going

place

could

so

 Read the story.
Find answers in the story.

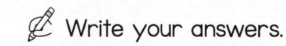 Read each question.
Write your answers.

A Day at the Farm

My grandpa lives on a farm. We are going to see him. The farm is a fun place to visit. I get to help feed the animals. Sometimes grandpa lets me ride on the big, green tractor. I wish I could live on the farm too. It is so much fun!

1. Who lives on a farm?

_____

_ _

_____

2. What color is the tractor?

_____

_ _

_____

3. What do I help do on the farm?

_____

_ _

_____

Think about the story. What was the most important idea?

Main Idea

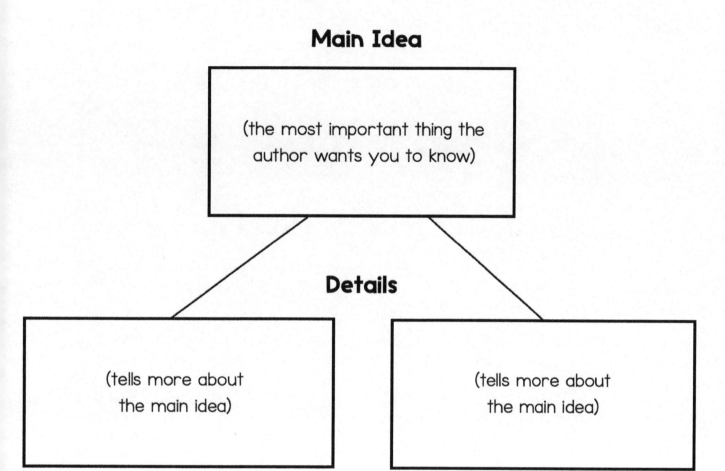

(the most important thing the author wants you to know)

Details

(tells more about the main idea)

(tells more about the main idea)

Directions:

 Cut out the statements.

 Glue them on the chart above to show which is the main idea and which are details..

Sometimes grandpa lets me ride on the big, green tractor.

I get to help feed the animals.

The farm is a fun place to visit.

STORY 7
A Good Pet

<u>Words to Practice</u>

have

good

they

very

you

want

A Good Pet

I have a pet named Ben. He is a mouse. A mouse makes a good pet. They are very quiet. They will not make noise when you sleep. Mice do not eat a lot of food. You can feed them things like apples and corn. If you want a good pet, get a mouse.

1. What kind of pet do I have?

    _____

    -

    _____

2. What is one food mice eat?

    _____

    -

    _____

3. What is my pet's name?

    _____

    -

    _____

Think about the story. What was the most important idea?

Main Idea

(the most important thing the author wants you to know)

Details

(tells more about the main idea)

(tells more about the main idea)

Directions:

 Cut out the statements.

 Glue them on the chart above to show which is the main idea and which are details..

Mice do not eat a lot of food.

They are very quiet.

A mouse makes a good pet.

STORY 8
Frogs and Toads

Words to Practice

are

they

live

different

also

have

 Read the story.

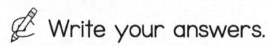 Read each question.

Find answers in the story.

Write your answers.

Frogs and Toads

Frogs and toads are not the same. They live in different places. Frogs live by the water. A toad lives on land. They also look different. Frogs have smooth, wet skin. Toad skin is dry and bumpy. Frogs have long legs for jumping. Toads have short legs for hopping.

1. What kind of skin do toads have?

2. Which animal has long legs?

3. Where do frogs live?

Think about the story. What was the most important idea?

Main Idea

(the most important thing the author wants you to know)

Details

(tells more about the main idea)

(tells more about the main idea)

Directions:

 Cut out the statements.

 Glue them on the chart above to show which is the main idea and which are details..

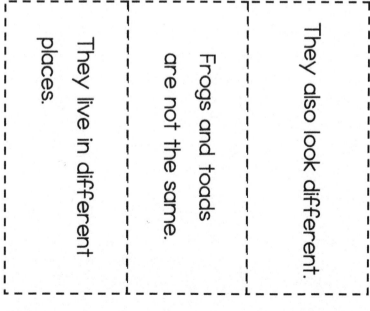

They live in different places.

Frogs and toads are not the same.

They also look different.

ANSWER KEYS

Rex's New Dog

Rex got a new dog. He loves to play with his dog. Sometimes Rex takes his dog to the park. They run and jump and chase each other. Rex throws a ball for his dog. Rex has fun with his new dog!

1. What did Rex get?

   Rex got a new dog.

2. What does Rex love to do?

   He loves to play with his dog.

3. Where does Rex take his dog?

   Rex takes his dog to the park.

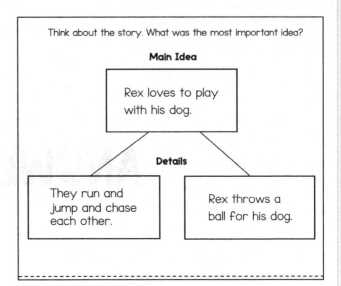

Think about the story. What was the most important idea?

Main Idea

Rex loves to play with his dog.

Details

They run and jump and chase each other.

Rex throws a ball for his dog.

*Note: The two supporting details for each story can be glued into either box. The order does not matter. The goal is for the child to discern between main idea and details.

A Snowy Day

It is snowy and cold. Jen wants to go outside and play. She has to get ready first. Jen goes to her room to get her boots. Next, Jen puts on a hat and her coat. Now Jen is ready to go out and play in the snow.

1. Where does Jen want to go?

   Jen wants to go outside.

2. What is the weather?

   It is snowy and cold.

3. Where are Jen's boots?

   Jen's boots are in her room.

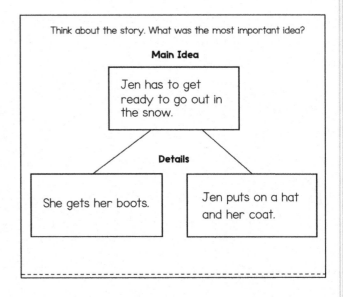

Think about the story. What was the most important idea?

Main Idea

Jen has to get ready to go out in the snow.

Details

She gets her boots.

Jen puts on a hat and her coat.

📖 Read the story. ❓ Read each question.
🔍 Find answers in the story. ✏️ Write your answers.

Party at the Park

Today is my birthday. I will have a party at the park. The park is a good place for a party. My friends can run and play. We can have cake on the picnic bench. All the moms and dads can sit and talk. A park is the best place for a party.

1. Where can we have cake?

   on the picnic bench

2. Who can run and play?

   My friends can run and play.

3. Why am I having a party at the park?

   Today is my birthday.

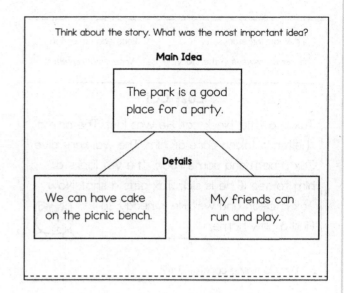

Think about the story. What was the most important idea?

Main Idea

The park is a good place for a party.

Details

We can have cake on the picnic bench.

My friends can run and play.

📖 Read the story. ❓ Read each question.
🔍 Find answers in the story. ✏️ Write your answers.

The Blue House

Mr. and Mrs. Tam had a green house. They do not like green. They wanted to paint the house. Mr. Tam went and got some paint. Mrs. Tam went and got some brushes. They painted all day. Now the house is blue!

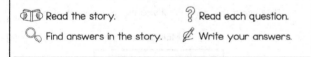

1. What did Mr. and Mrs. Tam want to do?

   They wanted to paint the house.

2. What did Mr. Tam get?

   Mr. Tam got some paint.

3. What color is the house now?

   Now the house is blue.

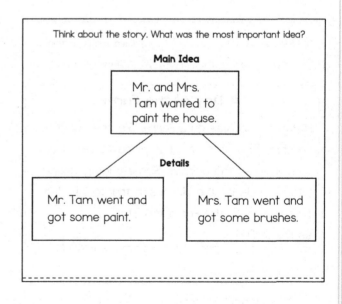

Think about the story. What was the most important idea?

Main Idea

Mr. and Mrs. Tam wanted to paint the house.

Details

Mr. Tam went and got some paint.

Mrs. Tam went and got some brushes.

📖 Read the story.   ❓ Read each question.
🔍 Find answers in the story.   ✏️ Write your answers.

Lost Cat

Jax is a little, black cat. He was lost. The animal shelter is taking care of him. The workers give Jax a bath and some food. The vet looks at him to see if he is sick. Jax gets a shot. Now Jax is clean and well. He is ready to find a new home.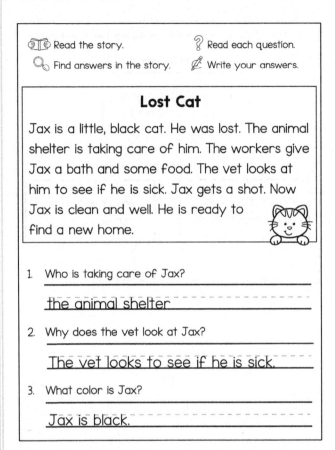

1. Who is taking care of Jax?

   the animal shelter

2. Why does the vet look at Jax?

   The vet looks to see if he is sick.

3. What color is Jax?

   Jax is black.

Think about the story. What was the most important idea?

Main Idea

The animal shelter is taking care of Jax.

Details

The workers give Jax a bath and some food.	The vet looks at him to see if he is sick.

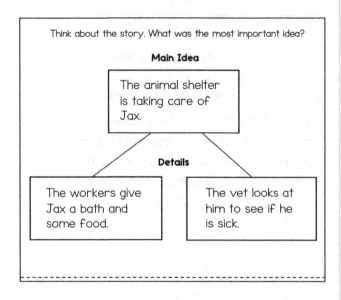

📖 Read the story.   ❓ Read each question.
🔍 Find answers in the story.   ✏️ Write your answers.

A Day at the Farm

My grandpa lives on a farm. We are going to see him. The farm is a fun place to visit. I get to help feed the animals. Sometimes grandpa lets me ride on the big, green tractor. I wish I could live on the farm too. It is so much fun!

1. Who lives on a farm?

   My grandpa lives on a farm.

2. What color is the tractor?

   The tractor is green.

3. What do I help do on the farm?

   I help feed the animals.

Think about the story. What was the most important idea?

Main Idea

The farm is a fun place to visit.

Details

I get to help feed the animals.	Sometimes grandpa lets me ride on the big, green tractor.

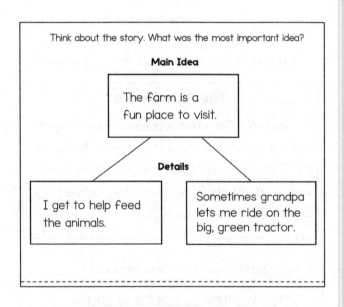

📖 Read the story.　　❓ Read each question.
🔍 Find answers in the story.　✍️ Write your answers.

A Good Pet

I have a pet named Ben. He is a mouse. A mouse makes a good pet. They are very quiet. They will not make noise when you sleep. Mice do not eat a lot of food. You can feed them things like apples and corn. If you want a good pet, get a mouse.

1. What kind of pet do I have?

   I have a mouse.

2. What is one food mice eat?

   apples OR corn

3. What is my pet's name?

   My pet is named Ben.

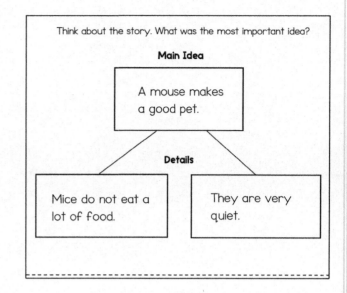

Think about the story. What was the most important idea?

Main Idea

A mouse makes a good pet.

Details

| Mice do not eat a lot of food. | They are very quiet. |

📖 Read the story.　　❓ Read each question.
🔍 Find answers in the story.　✍️ Write your answers.

Frogs and Toads

Frogs and toads are not the same. They live in different places. Frogs live by the water. A toad lives on land. They also look different. Frogs have smooth, wet skin. Toad skin is dry and bumpy. Frogs have long legs for jumping. Toads have short legs for hopping.

1. What kind of skin do toads have?

   Toad skin is dry and bumpy.

2. Which animal has long legs?

   Frogs have long legs.

3. Where do frogs live?

   Frogs live by the water.

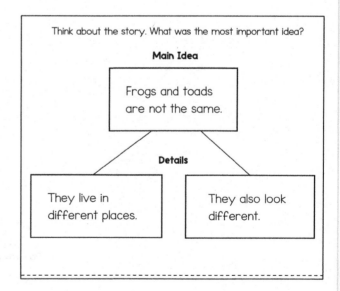

Think about the story. What was the most important idea?

Main Idea

Frogs and toads are not the same.

Details

| They live in different places. | They also look different. |

Made in the USA
Coppell, TX
06 November 2024